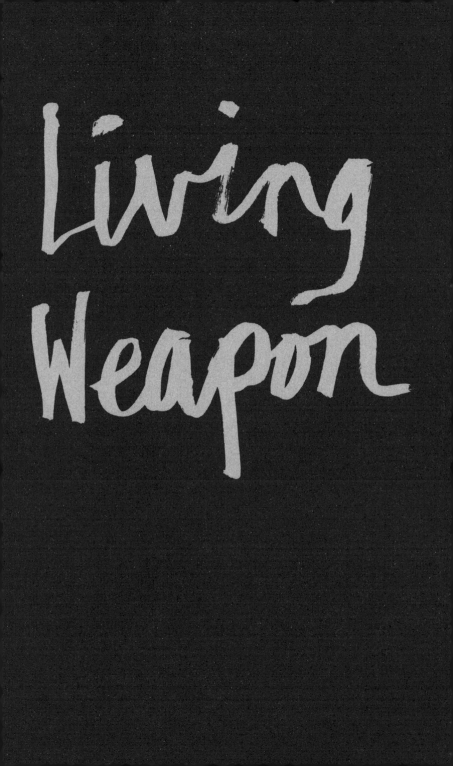

Living
Weapon

*Farrar, Straus and Giroux • New York*

# Living

ROWAN

RICARDO

# Weapon

PHILLIPS

Farrar, Straus and Giroux
120 Broadway, New York 10271

Grateful acknowledgment is made for permission to reprint lines
from "Credences of Summer," from *The Collected Poems of Wallace
Stevens*, by Wallace Stevens, copyright © 1954 by Wallace Stevens
and copyright renewed 1982 by Holly Stevens. Used by permission
of Alfred A. Knopf, an imprint of the Knopf Doubleday Publishing
Group, a division of Penguin Random House LLC. All rights reserved.

Library of Congress Cataloging-in-Publication Data
Names: Phillips, Rowan Ricardo, author.
Title: Living weapon / Rowan Ricardo Phillips.
Description: First edition. | New York : Farrar, Straus and Giroux, 2020.
Identifiers: LCCN 2019038070 | ISBN 9780374191993 (hardcover)
Subjects: LCGFT: Poetry.
Classification: LCC PS3616.H467 L58 2020 | DDC 811/.6—dc23
LC record available at https://lccn.loc.gov/2019038070

Designed by Crisis

Our books may be purchased in bulk for promotional,
educational, or business use. Please contact your local
bookseller or the Macmillan Corporate and Premium Sales
Department at 1-800-221-7945, extension 5442, or by
e-mail at MacmillanSpecialMarkets@macmillan.com.

www.fsgbooks.com
www.twitter.com/fsgbooks
www.facebook.com/fsgbooks

1 3 5 7 9 10 8 6 4 2

FOR NÚRIA, IMOGEN, AND ASTRID

Far in the woods they sang their unreal songs,
Secure. It was difficult to sing in face
Of the object. The singers had to avert themselves
Or else avert the object. Deep in the woods
They sang of summer in the common fields.

They sang desiring an object that was near,
In face of which desire no longer moved,
Nor made of itself that which it could not find . . .
Three times the concentrated self takes hold, three times
The thrice concentrated self, having possessed

The object, grips it in a savage scrutiny,
Once to make the captive, once to subjugate
Or yield to subjugation, once to proclaim
The meaning of the capture, this hard prize,
Fully made, fully apparent, fully found.

**WALLACE STEVENS**

*I ain't scared of none of this.*

JESSICA CARE MOORE

# CONTENTS

## 1776

Early on the hottest day of the year, in the black but thinning darkness of morning, I saw the top of the new skyscraper peek through the gauze of lingering night's sleepy electric glaze.

There it was, 1776 feet in the air.

We looked at each other like lightning in far-off fog.

Yeah, the spire looked at me, too.

All things this high up in the air have a living quality to them, how they move oh so slightly in the upper atmosphere as though breathing or, at the very least, being breathed into.

Either life-in-death or death-in-life, maybe someday it'll seem simply itself—Freedom Tower: half in shadow and half in light under a typically starless and purpled New York City sky.

It's four in the morning and I've put my faith in being unseen now among the low iron clouds.

At this hour, who looks up into the sky?

Drained by the sleep of millions of dreamers, the un-plugged skyline sleeps dull and firm.

The winds work their way up the tower's panes of glass like fingers on the fret board of a guitar. This is the breathing thing I was talking about earlier.

The winds up here enthuse everything to life.

But immediately after they pass, nothing happens.

Then, after that dead pause, the spire sways ever so slightly and the infinitesimally small torque of the metal moans.

I shift in the air, turning from the blank pages of the ocean to face the scrawl of the city's rooftops as they span out toward uptown, the suburbs, and beyond into blackness.

Pure silence.

Impure silence.

Pure silence.

Just a few miles ahead I can see Central Park, the dark, se-cretive rectangle at the heart of Manhattan.

Lit streets run from it, electric arteries and veins. Manhattan's never seemed so empty, so narrow, a pupil of a cat's eye.

I breathe in deeply.

I needed this.

Suddenly, a murmuration of starlings shoots up into the air from the park's dozing treetops. A lithe, twittering black cloud that climbs the dark sky, twists even further upwards, and then darts down and across to the side.

I've seen the sinuous back of a black panther scale that skywall and felt less afraid then, less alone midst the clouds than I do now as I watch the flying mass veer toward Harlem, then toward New Jersey, before bending back over the park and then out over the Atlantic, still surging, still together, past the limits of my vast sight, chorusing to the invisible countries in the receding horizon. A bone-old solitude creeps into my head and settles inside my wings.

Hovering here, I thought for once to try to remember it all; I thought this would be a remarkable moment . . .

but do I sound remarkable to you?

I can say things like

*The tower's spire was a lancet that drew me out of a cloud like a drug*

or

*I am a drop of blood from the tip of Heaven's finger*

Things I tell myself to feel better about these pointless joyrides. But in the end, that's all that they've been. Pointless joyrides.

I make nothing happen.

Especially at 1776 feet in the air.

I've done 1776 before. I've even been higher than that. Oh, I've been much higher than that. Once, I reached the end of the lowest ring of the Earth's atmosphere, the thinning upper ether where there's nowhere to rest, no perch to catch your breath, and hardly any air to breathe in even if there was a perch on which to catch your breath. I flew so high up that the sky itself ended. The stars turned pink and throbbed. There's an impossible music in the air at this height: the faint, purring expansion of all things cupped to your ear. The champagne of sound. But there was nothing to do up there. Eventually, I needed to either give in to gravity and come down, or let my momentum continue to pull me up into the freezing burn and the blinding white drift of the stratosphere, rising without end until I eventually drowned in space.

So I fought nature and descended. Quicker than I ever had before, I descended out of control and out of options. And as I descended, it was then that I saw for the first time the top of the new tower. As I approached it, I fell in an uneasy zigzag, involuntary changes of pace pushed and pulled me as I darted down in a scratched line like lightning does. I felt split in half. My wings were scorched at their highest points, the arches smoldered, ice ran down the sides to the sharp tips at the bottom. I like to say that I never get nervous, that I've never panicked in my life, that my nervous system is predisposed to tranquility, a constant correction of the checks and balances in the body and mind that render me phlegmatic and aloof. *If you have to do something anyway*, I've heard myself say time after time, *why bother panicking?* But for the first time that I can remember, I felt hysteria lap my blood. I flapped all of me—arms, legs, wings—I flapped all of me like a feral animal. My mother says this is how I came into the world.

What calms you when shit hits the fan? Me? I start to hum some Beethoven, *Heiliger Dankgesang*, the third movement from the A Minor quartet. It was tough to remember how it began with the cold music of the void of space still in my head. I was desperate to remember something utterly human. And given how we all make art with the same material—time, art is made of time—

there's something desperately human about music. That it's sound set to time. And time only exists in our paltry sense of ourselves. Time is what makes us and limits us. Music is what remakes us and expands us.

Four notes in I tucked my elbows into my ribs so that my forearms extended out from the sides of my torso and I began to wade my hands through the cloudburst as I dropped to the small landing spot on the spire. Hands hip-high in the speed of the gales, slightly twisting my palms up and then down, I slowed, though still descended; I regained control, descending then as though I wasn't moving at all.

> *. . . eighteen hundred and sixty-eight . . .*
> *. . . eighteen hundred and sixty-five . . .*
> *. . . seventeen hundred and ninety-one . . .*
> *. . . seventeen hundred and eighty-seven . . .*
> *. . . seventeen hundred and seventy-six . . .*

My feet felt for a landing, found it, and touched down on the cold nub. Like a gargoyle. I crouched down and rested my hands beside my feet to better balance myself. The intense warmth of the red light emanating from the beacon surprised me. It made me red all over and everything I saw from that perch was also filtered deep red.

Everything changed: the expanses of city and sky encrimsoned, all things corralled in a dark coral glow as though a red mist had descended on me.

That's when I launched myself from the spire.

Flight is like untying the air itself, fold after fold and layer after layer until there's nothing left to unwrap, and just like that you find yourself floating. I try to never take it for granted. I try to remember that at any moment this could all end. But there are people who like to say

> *I wish I were free, as free as a bird or as free as the wind*

and am I supposed to be that? For them? Am I supposed to never have felt as free in my life as I do here in the air, even though I have?

Freedom, when it doesn't feel the lyrics, is an unconvincing singer.

It's taken me years to find a safe altitude where I could think things through, contemplate the world, my country, my city, myself, high enough to be out of clear sight from the ground, low enough to remain off the agendas of radar and out of the paths of planes. Here is where I can be me, whatever I am. Here: this cramped corridor of New York City sky between Governors Island, Staten Island, Red Hook, and the Financial District. Here where the air is callus-thick. I circle in it like the contents of a Magic 8-Ball coursing between extremes.

The first blue aspects of the sky at this hour are unreasonably beautiful, like the color of that color in a cube of ice. These twenty seconds of flight, like Yeats's twenty minutes in "Vacillation" of feeling blessed and being able to bless in the embrace of such utterly fleeting happiness . . .

. . . but seven seconds into that feeling and the achingly early morning traffic has already begun to seep through the solitude.

Fourteen feet of wings tucked into the back of a jacket, a restraining strap squeezed around my trunk, passing for some acceptable version of normal, walking with you, working with you. I try these days to just enjoy it. And to see what grows from it.

So this one isn't about being born with wings; or about the eleven times my parents or I tried to cut them off only to feel them growing back longer and more resilient to the blade. This one isn't about the new tower in the invisible shadows of the old towers. This one isn't about this flight, this isolated twenty-second flight in the morning of nautical twilight. And isn't that enough? Doesn't every heart have somewhere deep inside of it a nocturnal lover who sleeps like a cereus inside its darkened core, and rises like a savage sun that crawls out from its cave and stands tall on the horizon?

Slowly, I rose to my feet, adding myself to the tower's height, and waited there for day to break, for the sun to rise, and for that one moment in the dawn when the light takes measure of us and welcomes us to the machine.

That on the silent horizon, something
Not a sunrise rose, half itself and half
The horizon, dragging its bulk, its lights
And salts, from under shifting sheets of sea,
Leveling the sky into shallow moats
Of sounds, flecks of birds, beginning again
To believe all brief and sideways dreaming
To be, as previous was the complaint,
Lint on time's black coat, blanketing the west,
Becoming the unfathomable death mask
Freckled with stars, rendering itself
As its other, as though to mirror la,
But not mirroring it, and therefore now
Mirroring it, all sumptuous unscripted
La, la mirroring la like the pricked prong
Of a tuning fork that, for all its song,
Between sensation and sensation is
Still nothing but air, a titan's dying
Air, a titan's dying air now again

A titan's surging flame, an ancient flinch
In an ancient sun mirrored and made
Into la, the void in the voice, the voice
In the void, lala: aiai, song and pain,
Song and pain, song and pain, and there it is.

# VIOLINS

He never saw a violin.
But he saw a lifetime of violence.

This is not to presume
That if he had simply seen

A violin he would have seen
Less violence. Or that living among

Violins, as though they were
Boulangeries or toppling stacks

Of other glazed goods like young adult
Fiction, would have made the violence

Less crack and more cocaine,
Less of course and more why god oh why.

More of one thing
Doesn't rhyme with one thing.

A swill of stars doesn't rhyme
With star. A posse of poets doesn't rhyme

With poet. We are all in prison.
This is the brutal lesson of the twenty-first century,

Swilled like a sour stone
Through the vein of the beast

Who watches you while you eat;
Our eternal host, the chummed fiddler,

The better tomorrow,
MCMXVI.

# HISTORY

It's late. History promises you a kiss
When she comes to bed. So you say good night.
You're tired and can't keep your eyes open,
So you called it surprisingly early.

She, like every night this summer, stays up
To watch her shows. Later, she woke you,
Accidentally, with a light you thought was
Dawn but was just the white haze of her cell.

You stayed half-awake in the lit darkness
Thinking she owed you something: a mere kiss,
Waiting, one eye half-open, like the flesh
In a shell sensing a swimmer pass—.

The light turned off as if it never happened.
And nothing came to you because you were
Owed absolutely nothing. Not even
The growing indifference in her voice.

# HALO

We wander round ring after ring of life,
One after another, blossoms of light
To which we're but a mere flotsam of bees.

And although this isn't true, the poem says
This is true; life, light, flowers, and bee: truths.
So stop and hold this poem above your head.

Hold it up to whatever light you find.
Then let it go: forget it, if you can.
If it is meant to remain it will remain.

And if it is meant to light, it will light.
Your hands will have moved on to something else
But your head will have, say it, its halo.

# MORTALITY ODE

Waiting in the cellular store like waiting for bread
We see two NYC police cars pull up, casually,
One behind the other. Two officers enter,
Two wait outside. One struts up and stops
A few feet from the counter and leans
Forward, like a dark blue crane. The person at the front
Of the line, over whose shoulder he makes concrete
The coarse abstraction of his presence, doesn't turn.
The woman behind the counter asks the officer for his
    name, which begins
With Officer, she tells him he's now in the system,
She'll call him when it's his turn, to make himself
Comfortable. The other officers come in then.
They begin fidgeting with the phones on display
And talk about those things they feel they can talk about
Suddenly public in their public service,
Hemmed in with the rest of us cut off from
Communication, worldless. I have no idea how much time
Has passed now: I don't have my phone; well over

An hour: I feel a creeping hunger. Anyway,
One of them breaks away from the conversation
For another compulsory round of seeming like
He has something to do. Grim-waisted, he dawdles
Past the digital tablets and begins testing the weight
Of oversized smartphones and smartphones small enough
To fit in a watch, his right hand hip-high
And resting on the pimpled, black, blunt
End of his piece as he walks, like all of them,
Unbalanced but propped up by strange gravity now visible,
A monochrome, unearned elegance.
He orbits us, curious for a moment about
His future, about what will be in his hand when
It's not reaching into a holster, when he checks the weather
And wonders what in the world to wear.
I watch him pass by the inventory on display twice
Before he slowly strides over to the glass window
In the back corner of the store where a solitary engineer
Tinkers with unresponsive hardware clinging to life.
He leans forward the way his partner did as though he is
Learning something or remembering something
Or being someone learning something or
Remembering something, his right hand lifting
From the dead metal and meeting his left on
The blue ledge of the swing door shut tight just below

The window, locking his fingers together, arms
Akimbo, his badge now caught on the edge like a wedge,
And then, just as it looked like his nose might touch
The glass, the guy who's been helping me, who'd
    disappeared into
Those mysteries of the back, the shelves of stock,
Bouquets of crumpled stuff, the Shangri-la of the staff
    john,
Emerges from an unseen door and asks the officer
If he can pass; sure, the officer says
And the brother makes a beeline to me, my phone is
Finally ready, it took a while to transfer all the content
To the upgrade, lots of data, but I'm all set now, he says.
I turn the phone on: the black screen ignites, singing
A single, held passion note, a pretense
Of life, then stops, revealing my home
Screen. Everything I had before looks up at me now
From the sleek mirage of short-lived newness,
Short-lived lightness, but it's pretty, though. True.
    Thanks.
The officers are reunited now, huddled like gum, close-
    knit
But silent, their wall mended. I open my phone's camera
To sneak a picture of them.
Because it's four cops in a cell phone store.

I lift my phone nowhere near their direction

As though I'm simply testing its weight

While straining, subtly, to center them in the aim.

The blurs flame then suddenly flare and come into focus when

The guy who's been helping me, without looking up

From his monitor, his hands still resting on

His keyboard like hands holding the end of a net,

Asks me—his voice quick as a Camaro—

If I think I'll want protection for that

Because you never know: you never ever know.

## SPIEGEL IM SPIEGEL

I swept away the heaps of broken glass
But I don't know where they went after that.
A repurposed, resurfaced Heaven perhaps

With its extra syllable for good luck
Like the way Spanish adds a rogue breath tucked
In front of the *s* in English words, "start"

Becoming then "estart" and "Spider-man"
"Espider-man" as though the sad human
Sound that the snake makes could be saved from sin

By a little, inhaled inspiration,
Not a tech title—epoem, eRowan—
But rather a reminder of why sun

After sun after sun after sun comes
Back to us slightly more cracked at the core;
Because experience is translation

Of an event we were all a part of:
When the young, lonely god took the gloves off,
Shattered the black mirror, and called it love.

## THE LUNATIC, THE LOVER,
## AND THE POET

And, after the explosion made spheres sing:
A pure expression of pure poetry.
Like rising rain or a nation with no
Flag—. Something that whispers as the air
Does just before the lightning comes. A pure
Expression of the breaks in the blank lakes
On Neptune's moons. A ruined expression
Of pure poetry. A pure expression
Of ruined poetry. Either will do.
A pure expression of pure poetry
In the podcasts of the pine trees will do.
We will say we do not want it because
We will say we do not want it because.
A pure expression of pure poetry
That boiled in the blur of the first atom.

There's a screen to tell you what pleasure is,
Who pleasure is, when pleasure is, and why.
You hold it in your hand and feel all things
As though the sheer, unseen rings of Neptune,
Blue-hued, were spinning there in your hand.
Look up from this poem and you will see
The long work of chaos and order cooled
Into this perceivable form of life,
Something manageable from the bow shock,
Where the end of the Earth's influence bends
Like a bow of light across the awful
Endlessness of the ever-cold ether.
The long work of chaos and order plugged
Into something else that's plugged into
Something else that's plugged into the air.
You play Kevin Bacon with it until
It bends like the first flare of plasma bent.
A pure expression of pure poetry.

The world is on fire. I see you across
A moving haze of invisible flames
That blurs the bruised mind to melisma.
The scream is closer. The magma sky, too.
A man hauls crate after crate of rifles
Into a hotel. A child is shot dead
On the spot as he plays with a toy gun
In a park. Some small-town lawyer calls
The melting world a myth and yet believes
In prayer, that God hears and cares for him
And somehow, amid thirteen billion years
Of stars to care for, has time for his shit.
What's the difference, if not love? And where did
It all go so, so wrong? I remember
You, nose to nose in the Bang, holding on.

## THOUGHTS AND PRAYERS

And so, what comes after heaven that's not
Heaven? Even Lucifer, having been
Hollowed out by lightning, cored by it, still
Called the sour sulfide lakes and charred meadows
That sprang up there, the dungscape, the sky tiled
With its constellate of apostate dead,
All this Lucifer still called Heaven.
And so, what comes after Heaven
If not itself? The end then is always
Just the beginning of the end of that end.
This is when we discover what evil
Really is: the end of endings; the death
Of change; that moment when you survey
What has fallen into your range of sight
And say this is good enough, this will do.

# NOVEMBER NOCTURNE

I looked out over the cool rising night,
Its soft froth of lamplight and scrubbed-out stars
Tumbling out over the blue tub, mind's sky,
Cash-only bars, evening everlasting,
Triumphant Brooklyn barely visible
Tucked behind the East River like the hem
Let out of an iridescent dress culled
To continue being the verse, the harm,
The wine-tonned mouth swollen with the last words
Of Spring or April or Night or The Plain
Sense of Things, the worlds in it burning, ways
Of I am now burning, feeling the Bern
In the back of a cab without being burned,
Then being burned. I wonder what I learned.

Then, Seamus Heaney's poem—suddenly—gone,
The words became a thing looked at, not read.
But then those, too, went the way of Patrón,
Blanketing whatever dim light November
Had let in. In the poem's place an oyster
Appeared on a plate: languid, the color
Of vanilla, moist fennel, raw silver,
Crushed hay, sunk ships, quince, and Jupiter,
Flexing taut, then slack, then taut in its shell;
How, with all that had happened, it managed
To be there, the gorged bulb glistening, well,
Here's where I'd tell you . . . but a ghoulish
Creamsicle flavor ruined the moment,
A sad irrelevance now relevant.

When equality feels like oppression,
The keyboard like a sword and a cannon,
And the comfort of being everyone
Or not (which you learned without learning it)
Fooling you into thinking that you're brave,
No, bored. It wasn't quite football season
Yet, was it? And there was Charlottesville,
Flickering like a pixel in *The Legend*
*Of Zelda*. You dreamt of being there: cool
In the crowd, your matching tiki torches
Almost touching in the trolling twilight.
A Southern Cross and someone dumb enough
To drive the car. Wake up! We've sent tin cans
Past Neptune. It's the twenty-first century.

# WHO IS LESS THAN A VAPOR?

*—after Donne's Meditation XII*

What won't end a life if a vapor will?
If this poem were a violent shaking of
The air by thunder or by cannon, in
That case the air would be condensed above
The thickness of water, of water baked
Into ice, almost petrified, almost
Made stone and no wonder; no la. But that
Which is but a vapor, and a vapor
Not exhaled when breathed in, who would not think
Miserably then, put into the hands
Of nature, which doesn't only set us
Up as a mark for others to shoot at,
But delights itself in blowing us up
Like a glass, till it see us break, even
From its own breath? Madness over madness
Misplaced, overestimating ourselves
Proceeding ourselves, we proceed from ourselves
So that a self is in the plot, and we
Are not only passive, but active, too,

In this destruction contract. Doesn't my
Calling call for that? We have heard of death
On these small occasions and from unearthed
Instruments: a pin, a comb, a hair yanked,
A golden vision gangrened and killed. But
Still the vapor. Still. So, if asked again, What
Is a vapor? I couldn't tell you. So
So insensible a thing; so near such
Nothings that reduce us to nothing.
And yet for all their privileges, they are
Not privileged from our misery; for they
Are the vapors most natural to us,
Arising in our own bodies, arising
In the clot-shine of disheveled rumor;
And those that wound nations most arise
At home. What ill air to meet in the street.
What comes for your throat like homebred vapor,
Comes for your throat as Fugitive, as Fox,
As Soulman of any foreign state. As
Detractor, as Libeler, as Scornful Jester
At home? For, as they babble of poisons
And of wild creatures naturally disposed
(But of course) to ruin you, ask yourself
About the flea, the viper; for the flea,
Though it may kill no one, does all the harm

It can, not so that it may live but so
That it may live as itself, shrugging through
Your blood; but the Jester, whose head is full
Of vapor, draws vapor from your head, pulls
Pigeons from his pockets, blares what venom
He may have as though he were the Viper,
As though he is not less than a Vapor,
As though there is no virtue in Power,
Having it, and not doing any harm.

# EPPUR SI MUOVE

Here's where things get weird: Why's it that we care?
Why can't we turn it off? And why's my mind
Like this? *Time is time*, I tell myself here
Where I can breathe, pause, and think: *time is time*,
*This moment is a gift.* But platitudes
Like these are full of shit. Time is not time.
This moment sucks. Trust is not trust. The rules
Of the world, that words mean things, that the mind
Will be the one sign of us to remain,
They couldn't care less anymore, you said.
We got it wrong, then right, then wrong again,
Being unprepared to play or be played.
We'd stretched ourselves across a wooden cross
That in the end was just a wooden cross.

# TRADITION AND THE
# INDIVIDUAL TALENT

I wandered through each chartered street
Till I was shot by the police.

# THE PEACOCK

Music for when the music is over
Is what a poem is. There's no music
In a poem, just the imaginary
Composer breathing beneath the deep wreck,
The curves of that glorious alphabet
Resilient as bioluminescence
Stuck in the seafloor. There's something to it:
How poems pretend to sing. As a peacock
Pretends in the wide span of its plumage
That there's no end to it: the far stars
Of galaxies and its ocelli gaze,
Gazed and gazing as one, the first fissions
Finally arriving at the listener,
Who makes sense of it sooner or later.

## A TALE OF TWO CITIES

City above the city and city
Below. The diners, theaters, bodegas,
Dance spots, and dives, all late-light strobed life
Sumptuous as solitude that knows it's not
Loneliness, like the blue blue-green peacock
Who gales open, waits, doubts, and then does not doubt.
There is a city above this city
And a city below this city: sky,
And you are the sky to it; and these buildings,
Iridescent in thick night like flora
And fauna, are its clouds. We all are part
Of another life's constellation,
A chanced-on font you see on a marquee
When you look out and then up,
When you think the thought that gets caught in air
And rises from your head like steam in the thaw:
That is the city above the city
Calling out to you through the blued spectrum,
That veiled feeling you keep to yourself of

The time you stood on a street and could swear
Some treasured part of you, that bird of fire,
Had just turned into a fish, and opened
Up, and surged upwards from below into
The darkness, the light, the darkness, the light,
The darkness, the light, the darkness, the light.

# TRINIDADIAN TRIPTYCH

*I. After a Lime on Ariapita Avenue*

The Trinidadian high court justice
Drives me back to my hotel. He's a poet.
He worries about the weight of the lives
In his hands. He worries about the weight
Of the words in our poems. We've been drinking
Since the sun isinglassed the ridged blue slope
Of the Queen's Park Cricket Club, the sinking
Birds cracking the pitch with their caws. A poem
Is a canary wincing its way down
A mine lost to time, answered the poem.
He is a good man. Our friendship has grown.
And poetry continues as it is
Because because because because because because
  because.

## II. Hart and Abercromby Étude

The Old Fire Station I'm sitting in
Near Woodford Square in downtown Port of Spain
Is lightly decorated inside by ten
Chinese lanterns swaying in the AC.
They dangle down from the ceiling's chipped slats.
I have absolutely no idea if
This answers your question. I'm where the streets
Hart and Abercromby meet. And love of
This, in its supreme and singular is,
The idea instead of the fact, its feel
Instead of what ___ finds when ___ googles
It, the ambered pinkish-brown soul sung real,
You ask as though you don't know what it is,
Play dead, let everything become ISIS.

*III. Swimmers in the Caribbean on the Eve of a Referendum*

A morning swim with Gemma Robinson
The day we're all set to leave Port of Spain.
Hannah Lowe nearby in a pool chair; sun
Everywhere and nowhere under light rain.
I float on my back, blazed, so many poems.
The sky seems more silver than gray. Gemma
Emerges and circles back to the edge, toes
Over the deep end of the pool again.
She bends at the waist, hands clasped in prayer,
Leans forward, and dives into the water.
Soon, she'll be back in Scotland. And Hannah
In London. With the referendum
Ripening and rotting. And Orpheus,
Who stayed behind, trapped like the three of us.

Yesterday's newspaper becomes last week's
Newspapers spread like a handheld fan
In front of the face of the apartment
Door. A dog does the Argos-thing inside,
Waiting beside O as though his body
Is but an Ithaca awaiting the soul's
Return. Neil the Super will soon come up
With the key but only in time to find
Doreen, the on-the-down-low friend-with-perks,
Already there, kneeling between the two,
Stroking the hair of both O and the dog,
Wondering who had been walking the dog.

# CRISIS ON INFINITE EARTHS

There's the idea you should love someone—
And the idea you have fallen in love.
Both are just ideas. Both a cosmic con.
I enjoyed thinking I was above
Such things: that love was option and choice.
So if I were to love someone, or fall
In love with someone, it was more a yes
To my selves across the void, as though all
My life were one multiverse-spanning dash
After another in search of that man.
I loved like this until I turned to ash.
I turned to ash just like the Flash. I ran
So fast I turned into a wasn't. Like
Love ground down by the love it loved to love.

# NUDE FIGURE

A blue sleeveless blouse with a gold zipper
Voilàing down the middle of the front,
Like the evening star that seems too supple
To move in any direction other
Than north and south against night's writhing silk;
My mind is the last panther in the hills
Haunched on a steep rock, drinking in that sky,
And all I once knew of the world now fills
With lies and fear and terror, flies past us
And dies as you lie back, the last sentence
Ever spoken in the lost tongue of the poets
That went, *This was our planet, a past tense,*
*Some dot gerrymandered into fire;*
*Douse it with tequila, chase it with rye.*

# THE TESTAMENT OF ORPHEUS

You start to tell me, then you simply tell me.
And as soon as you do you disappear
From the cab. It happened so quickly,
The turn. I remember you singing, *Here*
*I am and my body is, my mind is*
*All labyrinth laired with trillium and word*
*And sun and moon and echo and* I think
To keep going but shut the hell up, fold
Back into the cab, and close the door.
This is not about us. The drained sky meets
The drained moon in a compromise of dawn.
We are the morning's lingering lamplights
Mulling lullabies in our useless heads.
And love is the sun's power as it spreads.

# PURPLE ELEGY

Dearly beloved, this is what it sounds like
When you become a symbol through sound
That roreth of the crying and the soun:
You give up all your shit, down to the last sou,
Wade through raspberry death to find him and
Remind yourself he once was.

## EVEN HOMER NODS

You can be a mother who knows a god.
And you can ask him for magic armor,
A shield the width of Saturn's widest rings,
Some helmet in the new or ancient style,
Fill your arms with defenses for your child,
Take the peacock feather you've been offered
And plant it in that helmet's crown, or keep it
For yourself to use as a pen, note this
Was the only option you were offered,
Stylist or witness, witness with stylus,
So that you'd circle down the drain with death,
Mourning in either silence or sound bites,
Surrounded by silence and sound bites, life
Like this having been polished to shine
In the normal ways things shine these days,
A dull lull, the type of insufficient glare
We used to call out on sight as useless
Glow but now in new darkness we feel a need
For, a consolation of presence,

As when my mother passed me the soft shield,
The breastplate like rice paper, the helmet
Bright as pyrite can be, we already
Knew that this was part of the old cycle,
That I would die soon, without a weapon,
And she'd live on, and we'd do this again
And again and again, without ever
Knowing we were the weapon ourselves,
Stronger than steel, story, and hydrogen,
Here in America, where we wonder,
Still, after everything that's happened, why
Anyone bothers to read the classics.

## LOVE SONG

Not who or what you love, but that you love.
That to stand there or sit there, to simply
Be: this is hard. To look across from you,
Where someone else or no one or both may
Or may not be: this is hard. This is hard
Because you love and have learned not to love.
You say love, say you're filled with love;
Even to the edge of doom and all that.
But how perverse and proximal hate can be,
Like a volcano emptying itself
Onto the small town sprouting in its shade;
Hate ruling your continent, hate burning
Your air, hate sitting beside you under
A perfect moon, leaning in like love would
As the moon fades into the blue whiteness
Of dawn. We all share that awed silence while
The woke birds sing. We are all savages.

Wait. So you're new? Great.

I've always wanted to show someone around.

Here: If you look straight up you'll see

The tops of skyscrapers

Staring straight down

And the sidewalks you thought you were walking on

Are actually way up there in the high distance.

I know, right? Look at them,

All like the concrete vapor trails of thousands

Of concrete passing planes, and here, look down,

See your hands where your feet

Should be and nothing where your hands

Should be and nothing in your pockets anyway?

Awesome. Welcome to The First Light. Enjoy

The feeling while it lasts.

Because soon this will all be normal to you

And you will feel as normal as *&#%

And believe me that will #$*!&^@ suck. Look at this:

It's just like CGI. Touch me,

Oh, that's right: you have no hands.
Imagine touching me. It's much better that way
anyway. Anyway . . .
Yeah. No. It doesn't rain anymore. But
There's the sun up there maybe perhaps.
And every golden hour (I don't know what that is),
Like clockwork (I mean, right?), they
Have their people shake their trash cans
Out their windows
And the coins that make it down here
They feel kind of a little bit like rain.
They call it watering the money tree.
I'm just happy to be in the way.

# THE KÖLN CONCERT

Sunday morning, I woke for the first time
As a forty-three-year-old. Now I have a year
To get used to it. I'll likely forget
From time to time how old I am, and bear
A stunning resemblance to myself at
Forty-two when I didn't know a thing
About this poem, which suits this poem
Just fine because it's a poem of the soft
Future, like when a gloriously winged
Angel lands on top of Freedom Tower
We call that soft science fiction and move
On, remembering that I'm forty-three
When I have to face some kind of hard truth
About the spiraling shape of the past,
And the future starts to sound like the notes
In broken chords that haven't been played yet
But you know are coming because you think
Music is about agreement, even
If improvisation's the agreement;

And so, I realize now that I'm writing
In a key and that key is forty-three.
The last chord harmony of most pieces
Is what gives them their feeling of ending;
Otherwise, a song could potentially
Go on forever. The last chord provides
A sense of the writer's mood. Remember,
C Major and A Minor use the same
Notes. They're relations in different moods.
An upper. And a downer. Light. And dark.
The relative key of forty-three is
Maybe a subject for another time
When all life is *Heiliger Dankgesang*.
I've slid down the East Side of Manhattan
And settled in at the place where I work,
No, write, its knickknacks of a writer's life
Catch shine under the desk lamp like seashells.
On my desk, a bunch of tennis results
From 2017 and a few
Galaxies scribbled in black, red, orange,
And blue by Astrid, who'll turn forty soon
Enough in a provocation of sun.
Whether I'm here or not, I'll be eighty
By then. Whether I'm here or not, my face
Will be a fugue of stars. Was I not born

To be the pianist who moans and stomps
His feet under the tug of a chord's tide?
Years from now, when it's not a November
Afternoon and you don't look at the time
And don't feel like all the sunlight's been sucked
From all the air as though all the air is
Just the narrow bottom of someone's cup,
Remember what I'm now asking you here,
Because it wasn't a rhetorical
Question: I don't think I'm the pianist
Who moans and stomps his feet under the tug
Of a chord's tide, but there are mornings when
I wake up, drink coffee, make breakfast, read this
Or that, and then at some moment, alone with my age,
Silent in the awful silence of rage,
I wonder, surrounded by the silent
Applause of the monitor and the lamp,
What would have happened if, when I was twelve,
I didn't walk away from that Baldwin upright
I'd drop my head down on to hide my tears,
Those sharp black keys worn to matte and Rowan
Where he was supposed to be: Good, Rowan;
The Good Rowan; wake good Rowan up—
And tell him that the poet he hears trapped
In the ivory made it out, and lives.

# ÉTUDE ON MAN

How easy life made it to turn the words
Into a man. Blind-sugar being: man.
I took the five hooks from my mouth and said:
Be a man; justify the ways of God
To man; oh, man; etc. Maybe when I say
A man I really mean you or my mom
Or the blankness of blank verse blanking out
A name, likely some loose version of you
Or my mom but certainly not all this,
Which happens later. Disinterest in you
Grew. Man's mansong grew. Thus we related,
Erring. A cock in the hand was a red
Herring. Reading bore Stevens, Updike, Swift,
And Keith Haring but none of them voted
In the last election. My mind's not right.
I'll leave now. It's like stepping back from a
Shattered mirror. And then seeing it heal.

## THE KING OF THINGS

It wasn't a subject heading to trust:
"The Soul Holds No Treasure But For The Soul."
Nobody who means you well writes this way
In an email. You have to destroy it.
Sorry, you should delete it. That's the word.
For now on, let's use "delete" when we hate.
For now on, let's use "destroy" when we love.
We must destroy and then delete the soul.
Just in case. And when that soft side of you
To whom all wild messages are addressed
Opens your spammed life you will say nothing,
Because you should never say a damn thing.
The king of things, his worth, what you delete,
What you've destroyed, why you bother being,
Bothered being, just click here, and you'll know.

## THE QUESTION

When did you know you wanted to become
A poet? No one believes this question.
No one listens for the answer. It's one
Of those habits of people forced to live
Together on a spinning rock, the pale
Blue dot a wince in the wide attention
The dying light seeks out from ice giants
Dull and firm in the dark, under polite
Lights, midst rows and rows of people who ask
When and why about poetry, of she
Who forgets to ask something that was,
I realize later, part of the poem,
The part where it all comes together, and,
Having come together, finally sings.

# DARK MATTER ODE

You'll say you can't remember, you were too
Young—the idea wasn't yours. Or, maybe
You'll feel the need to feel misunderstood
And say, *You don't understand, You don't*
*Understand, You don't.* But I was there
When the sky closed. I know that brief darkness
Feels good. That God works on no sleep as certain
As Br'er Sleep reclining in your lampshade,
Sweet Br'er Sleep who never knows sleep. His song
Swells in my wrists as they hang on your crib.
Leaning in, inspecting you like a crook,
I am the poet in his pillory.
I see you as free. I sing of the wood.
And I sing of the bars. I am the dunce
Of the stars who sings of the bars.
Poets know time is a dead man walking:
We are all the terrorist Tichborne—.
I love that you sleep so softly despite
The virus of my verbal flailings flowing

Through your veins. One day you will be facing
It, the reflective black immensity
Of it all, and you will seethe and set out
Into a world of science and anger
I can't know or imagine. Today won't
Matter to you because today to you
Won't be today by then, which went like this:
There was the IMAX movie about Dark
Matter and the protests about how Black
Lives Matter, but then for you the same sleep
And then a million years from now someone
Will discover that something like this one
Moment could have happened, could have mattered,
That you asleep in your crib were a god
In the machine and that poem your father
Wrote you was a fucking living weapon.

# PORTRAIT

Barcelona. Early autumn. Warm enough for shorts: cool enough for sleeves.

The streets are full of people. Some in jackets, some in scarves, silk ones. They wear glasses with hard plastic frames the colors of scented sweets or fluorescent pistachios. The women don't care what the French do. No one bothers with the beach.

Soon there'll be the scent of chestnuts and soups on the streets. This smell, bright orange-brown with purple moods, is part of the transition from slow-to-unravel summer.

The pace of September was a compensatory one, everyone having returned from their vacations and the city once again ripe with life; the fast-twitch muscle of hope, the renewed crowds in one neighborhood after another—Sants, Eixample, Gràcia—now ballooning with purpose and tempo.

But then October opens like a creaky gate and reality walks back into your life. Real life untethered to whatever deals you made with yourself in the warm water and under a relentless sun. The stubborn last drops of summer's hot blood finally swabbed away, gleaned from the soul, the mind now practical again, fixed now again on what's real like bank accounts and bread, a memory-starved grandmother who waves you, the stranger, away. You hear October's creaking gate closing slowly behind you and zipper your jacket up to the base of your throat.

When you actually live in a place considered a paradise by tourists that place feels twelve degrees cooler for you than for the tourist. And the beach is strewn with them: tourists and expats. But Barcelona is no paradise. Barcelona is Boston with better weather. Barcelona is Boston if Boston had lost the war.

Today, a Thursday, the clouds are heavy and hot: they sag like a goddess reaching down to whisper into your ear that she favors you; they sag like the belly of a beer drinker in a tight white shirt. The clouds are hot and heavy on the bottom but light and cold up top. The clouds are stained with streaks of sun. It's sunny. It's not sunny. It's going to rain and it's not going to rain. Barcelona. Always betwixt and between. A quilt of old towns sewn together by culture, time, and a tongue. Its agnostic absence of right angles and the slight downhill slope of the boulevards bound for the sea sometimes leave me standing still when the rain comes down hardest, waiting for the flood.

That's what I'd been up to. Having taken the bus down Passeig Joan de Borbó to La Barceloneta. The blue-in-green parakeets have turned into white-in-gray seagulls that torque over the narrow streets. This is one of the few parts of Barcelona where the streets form a true grid. And despite the fact that there's no place in New York even slightly like here, that little bit of familiar order so close to the water puts me at ease. I imagine this is what a poet feels like when a poem is over. You feel your way through the lines like braille, forgetting for a moment the words.

It took no time at all for Barcelona to show me how lovely the bus can be for seeing the city. Back in New York, I avoided the bus. True, the subway may get you where you're going faster; you move through it like information moves through a wire. But riding the bus in Barcelona is like riding a slant of light. For the record, the buses and bus stops in Barcelona and New York are now exactly the same, the latter taking after the former. One of the best recent decisions made by Barcelona was to not try to be New York. No one decided it, but a type of unshakable communal common sense—the old Catalan *seny*—took over. Instead, New York has begun to pick up on things from Barcelona. And Catalans who want what New York have tended to go there and stay there. I guess Barcelona ended up with me in exchange, which must feel kind of depressing.

Because here I am now with nothing to do. And by doing nothing an idea came to me that I can finally put into motion. I'm trying to live, at least for a couple of hours, like a tourist again. I need it. I feel like I haven't spoken English in months, which may be why I'm writing all of this to you now. I've lost some words like, for example, "truss" (*braguer*). I find myself asking, "How do you say in English again . . . ?" You wouldn't think you could lose your first language, would you? But I am. And it frightens me.

The Barcelona bus system is great. It goes everywhere. And I mean everywhere. Once, I fell asleep on a bus and woke up in Sant Adrià de Besòs, on the outskirts of the city. I live on the very western edge of town, near the Camp Nou. Sant Adrià de Besòs is all the way on the other side of the city. When the jolt of motionlessness opened my eyes I didn't recognize a thing. The bus driver just sat in his seat with the bus idling. I could have been asleep at the last stop for five seconds or five minutes. Either he didn't care or assumed that I'd overslept my stop. I told him I'd overslept my stop and he said that, yeah, he kind of figured. I'm going to get going again back the other way in a minute.

I looked out the window I had been using as a pillow. Then out of the array of windows I had all to myself in the empty bus. The naked industrial void of the place, the perfunctory placement of things. This is where you buy your stuff, this is where you live, this is the spot not designed for you to hang out where you hang out, and this is the bus stop. Part of the naturally curious side of me suddenly died that day.

When I started to follow a couple that had just reached the roundabout with the Columbus statue as I made my way past the port, it wasn't anything I'd planned to do. It just happened. But what better way to live like a tourist than to spend time with tourists. Granted, I didn't ask them, but would they really mind? In the back of my head I hear myself—why lie? I hear myself in the front of my head and the back and all over—and think I sound like a suspect being interrogated by a detective. *It wasn't anything I had planned to do.*

They're from Orlando. No, they're from nearby Orlando: Kissimmee. Their conversation, first fuzzy, quickly comes into focus like a siren in the distance that grows louder as it reaches you and then stops right in front of you at full power.

The weather here compared to the weather in Orlando.

That there's a noticeable difference in the weather in Orlando and the weather in Kissimmee despite them being only seventeen miles apart.

Who would think that the weather in Orlando and the weather in Kissimmee would be different at all when they're so close to each other?

No one would think that the weather in Orlando and the weather in Kissimmee would be different at all because they're so close to each other.

Would you look at that?

El Mirador de Colom.

They followed Passeig de Colom to a large roundabout, one of many in the city. If the sea is Barcelona's legs and the mountains its head, Plaça de Catalunya its heart, then el Mirador de Colom, the Columbus statue, is its navel. It looks much better from afar than close up. This is in part because the actual statue stands high atop a column. Were they to keep going straight, crossing to the other end of the roundabout, they would have continued onto Passeig Josep Carner. Carner was a Republican known as the Prince of the Catalan Poets. Republican in the Spanish sense. It's become difficult to know when to elaborate on these things.

But we stop at Columbus.

The statue's such a clusterfuck that I don't even have at this point to pretend to be creeping on them. I go and stand right next to them, looking up at the Columbus Monument as they look up at the Columbus Monument. You have to look up the base, the plinth, the festival of the pedestal with its griffins and winged victories, all that allegorical brouhaha, and then past forty feet of Corinthian column to see him. Hard Columbus—gigantic and eternal, tricked out in pigeons, seagulls, verdigris, and palm trees—pointing in the wrong direction.

We then turn up Les Rambles and stroll toward the center of the city, the sea at our back. The scent of orange trees and palm trees, they say.

Barcelona. It's just as they dreamt it would be, they say, the orange trees and the palm trees, as though they were planted for them. They were planted for them.

It's all so Spanish. Every brunette with pearl earrings they see, if they had seen them, is the star of their expense. They walk with their arms locked, *Freewheelin'-Bob-Dylan*-album-cover style, suddenly simple folk in a city of the future, the caged parakeets for sale on each side of Les Rambles singing that they're for sale, plotting the same siren song every day so that the cage can open and one of them hidden in the corner, the unchosen one, can squeeze through, side-winged, and head for the north country. Portbou. Banyuls-sur-Mer. Collioure.

*What time are we meeting up with your friend?* His head still tilted and leaning on his wife's head as his lips move, a new perfume filling the spaces in his mouth the words came from, his eyes cautiously surveying everything he tries to look at with casual coolness.

*She said just text her whenever,* loving the moment but feeling a slight ache in her neck from supporting the weight of his head. *She's set aside today and the weekend for us.*

*Cool.*

They have a friend who moved here who knows when: Christine. She has two orange trees and a grapefruit tree growing in the small patch of ground just behind her tiled backyard. All the trees flowered and started to bear fruit. This year she watered them all just as she's done for the past seven years. But over the past two weeks, the fruit has started disappearing off the trees. She looks on the ground for the fallen fruit but never sees any. Her cats don't seem wiser than they otherwise would, they still circle her asking for their ground discs of failed meat and gristle so it's not them. She checked under her patio chairs, the corners of the yard, they may have all fallen and rolled here or there. She lives in Spain, near Barcelona, and the climate is good for growing this fruit. More than a quarter of the nation is unemployed. Could there be some animal or bird picking the fruit off the trees?

Tonight, they'll see a flamenco show with the other students in Christine's Spanish class. The couple will envy their friend's sandals though they're the same brand as theirs.

Positive charges, negative charges, millions of droplets of condensation corked in fat cumuli, microscopic mosaics of ice crystals moving without meaning. The blue and the gray tepid in the autumn air.

Cool.

Something something . . . which they've argued about before.

The resignation of it.

The implied sigh in the vowels, she squeezes his arm and reaches her chin up to kiss him without them breaking stride, then turns to look at the sights along the busy walkway, in part to look and in part to give her neck a break from the weight of his resting head.

The French will say "cool" at the drop of a hat, but the moment he heard it he knew he'd heard an American. I imagine I tried not to turn around, but I felt like Orpheus, the long-lost music of my past creeping up from behind me and turning my head.

I stopped dead in my tracks and turned to face them. *Whoa . . . haha . . . Easy there, guy.*

As though unlocking arms and splitting to go around would have sent them each off of separate cliffs, they picked up speed and veered around me, together, still clenched to each other but differently now, more urgently. Then they got right back on their course, slowing down again on their way toward Plaça Catalunya.

He shot a sizing glance back over his shoulder after they'd walked a reasonable distance, although he pretended he was turning his head just to kiss her again on top of hers. Columbus floated like a cursor just above me in the far air of the background.

I just stood there looking back at them. My blue Vancouver Canucks T-shirt peeking out from my unzipped jacket not having the ironic, uprooted affect on him that it has on everyone here. He looks at me—*French, I guess?* he thinks . . . *I don't know, whatever, just stop staring at us, man.* I caught a quick glimpse of a street hustler juggling a soda can like a soccer ball and when I looked back they had faded into the crowd.

I fall into these trances once in a while. It's when just the right syllable, American and corkscrewed, a "cool" or "hey," hits me weirdly, tragically off, like a plate in the face that was supposed to have pie on it. The moment, it sneaks up on me. It's when I'm not prepared, when I'm not perfectly from somewhere else that home swallows me whole and I freeze and my life, my beautiful life that I have built for myself here with its Mont Blanc pens, turns to smoke.

I've been having a go at Europe. I guess? I guess. I came to Barcelona for N. She's not the homesick type but there was an apartment. We shrugged our way to liquor stores and delis for boxes to use for packing our stuff, we shrugged our way to the post office to ship the hundreds of books we'd packed, we shrugged our way to friends' places to leave behind things not worth taking which meant just about everything else. Everyone understood. There was an apartment. We'd always been real-estate lucky. But it was stupid to spend all of that money shipping books.

I said I'd write something there. And I did. And then something else. And then something else after that. No one knew who I was. I became an acquired taste. No need to make a bildungsroman of it. This is why movies about artists tend to stink—they always attempt to make visible the wobbly space-time between the creator and the created. There's a reason we can't remember being born or the first few years of our lives we spend getting over it.

That redacted fragment of yourself is where the poems come from, when the greatest mystery of ourselves, how we learn our native language, happens indifferently and uninterested in its own mystery. Eventually, you arrive at an age and find a place where you can feel this part of you as it moves through you. And to your surprise, it sings to you in novels. Slim novels you couldn't put down, or you'd finish in a couple of days and give to a friend and ask them the next time you saw them if they'd read it and get on their case if they hadn't. Novels that sound like wrong chords at the right moment, clashing colors inked onto black-and-white photos. Urbane novels in the mannerist style with a posse of different-colored people busy being busy people.

You think, Yeah, I could do that.

But, as with most would-be writers, things didn't work out that way. You can blame, well not quite blame, but you can blame it on a series of accidents. Fatey things out of my control. But let's not get into that just yet. Here isn't the place for that. I have certain responsibilities toward you and I plan on meeting them.

I caught a cab in front of the Camp Nou. There's no game there tonight. Quarter-lit, the stadium sits there, starved of itself, like untouched cake, flags for each team stuck around the top rim like dwindled candles. I'm heading far enough off the beaten path that I have to give the driver a nearby location—the old hippodrome—and guide him the rest of the way from there. I don't play football, the taxi driver said. It takes a little while for the cabbie to find what he's looking for: the elevated main road that runs east-west along the northern part of town. But then he drives with confidence, the view opens up, and the city clears her throat.

The late-evening air is early-evening air here: it's just before eleven and I'm resigned to having dinner after the game. The game is on my mind. I don't feel the hunger. I don't feel the hunger enough to be mad about it. Sitting in the back of the cab in my game shorts, my legs look up at me after a full day under a desk. They flicker a livid orange with every streetlamp the cab passes, a bouncer's searchlights trying to coax a reaction from the traces of youth in the still slender muscle. I reach in my bag to make sure I have everything: fresh socks, musky shin guards, footwear for artificial turf, change of clothes, towel, and cell phone one by one and only once quickly as though they burned.

Positive thinking.

A positive thought.

Sky: the Mediterranean's jaded mirror heaves overhead in the dark. All faded indigo with a sheen of brown in it, the sparsely lit mountains in the distance, dusted with the distant lights of distant houses inching closer; the sea and noise of Les Rambles trailing behind him now like the tail of a kite as the cab rises and curves with the highway, then it hits that one straightaway the route offers and he floors it and pulls free.

I slump even further down in the back, disappearing completely from the rearview mirror like a black setting sun and close my eyes. My long, uncovered legs feel the squeeze of the faux-leather upholstery in front of me. No one is in front of me in the passenger's seat so I dig my knees as deep as I can into the back of the seat, stretch, and yawn.

The taxi is all mine now.

I roll my window down.

A cool wind roars inside the small dark interior; up front, I can hear loose sheets—a travel log, two news-papers—flapping then falling down into that space where one's feet would rest in the shadowed floor of the cab. We pass one residential street after another, turn toward Parc Güell as if it wasn't there, and keep on, for-ward, faster.

Nothing from here on is for the visitor.

The city's grid is gone now, the streets simply ending up where they need to. To the left, he sees how steep the streets become here, the hilly landscape surrendered to sparse concrete cash-grabs. To the right, the descending expanse of the city. The dark sea a liquid horizon at the end of the strings of the light of the night. Despite the endless apartment buildings, the hippodrome, the university so modern it looked dated the moment it opened, the university for tourism and hotel studies with the spotless subway station less than a decade old right next to it, these are the parts of Barcelona that never intended to be parts of Barcelona.

The car pulls up to the entrance of the parking lot. I tell the driver to enter the parking lot and pull up in the back where a walkway to the soccer fields begins. It's about to rain.

I pay and pop out of the car. I watch as the cabbie takes a long, wistful look around the lot and surrounding area for a potential fare all the way out here, but he sees none so slowly turns back toward the center resigned to his solitude and speeds away.

The high fences and concrete, the long unlit walkway ramp and the hard lights at the end of it. Even though I'm late I stand there for a few seconds. No one would confuse this for beautiful architecture or even brutally cool. But I smile and take a deep breath as though the sports complex were a cake fresh out of the oven. A strong trace of hashish kicks back at me and I laugh at my own ruined moment. It smothers me like barking chocolate. I don't know if I'm laughing at noticing the waft in the air or at not having noticed the two couples lighting up in the parked car twenty feet to my left. The two men are dressed as though they've just played; the two women dressed as though they've just had to sit through a game. They're listening to electronic dance music, the men in the front seats facing the back, passing the hash around like a peace pipe. They've been at this for years. What's natural becomes second nature.

The shrillest birdsong.

No: whistles.

Flocks of silver sounds rising simultaneously from the unsighted fields past the parking lot, over the high concrete wall in front of me, thrashing against the floodlight white-yellow haze humped over the vast stretches of synthetic grass like a giant phosphorescent shell on a turtle.

The whistles mean different things—

Once and short: foul.

Once and long: hold on, hold on . . .

Too many short ones to count: break it up, break it up, cut the bullshit.

Two medium ones followed by one long one: game over.

I start to walk toward game over.

Uphill toward the main walkway, past the first field on my right, past the lounge, past the smaller field, restaurant, and bar. Four more large fields appear. I see in the distance Field 6. No one else is there yet aside from the friendless referee, dawdling in the middle of the pitch, pretending he has something to do. I duck into the locker room and find my teammates, still in their street clothes, already talking politics. I ask Jordi if we're playing. He points outside and counts down. *Quatre . . . tres . . . dos . . . un . . .*

Then the clouds crack. Thunder pounds the ground. Lightning rakes the field. And we decide to vote on whether or not to wait it out.

## ACKNOWLEDGMENTS

Warm thanks to the editors of the following publications, where these poems, or earlier versions of these poems, first appeared: the Academy of American Poets' *Poem-a-Day* website, *The American Scholar*, *Black Renaissance/Renaissance Noire*, *The Common*, *The Cortland Review*, *GREY Magazine*, *The Harvard Advocate*, *Lana Turner*, *Literary Imagination*, *Little Star*, *The Nation*, *The Paris Review*, *The Paris Review Daily*, *Poetry*, *The Scores*, *Travel + Leisure*.

"The Golden Hour" was first published by the *Boston Review* in *What Nature*, edited by Timothy Donnelly, BK Fischer, and Stefania Heim.

"The First Last Light in the Sky" was republished by Scribner in *The Best American Poetry 2016*, edited by Edward Hirsch and David Lehman.

"Halo" was republished by Scribner in *The Best American Poetry 2017*, edited by Natasha Trethewey and David Lehman.

"Dark Matter Ode" was republished by Knopf in *Resistance, Rebellion, Life: 50 Poems Now*, edited by Amit Majmudar.